My Family at Work

My Grandfather Works in a Bakery

By Sarah Hughes

Children's Press
A Division of Scholastic Inc.
New York / Toronto / London / Auckland / Sydney
Mexico City / New Delhi / Hong Kong
Danbury, Connecticut

Thanks to The Bakery, New Paltz, NY

Photo Credits: Cover and all photos by Maura Boruchow
Contributing Editors: Jeri Cipriano, Jennifer Silate
Book Design: Michael DeLisio

Library of Congress Cataloging-in-Publication Data

Hughes, Sarah, 1964—
    My grandfather works in a bakery / by Sarah Hughes.
        p. cm. -— (My family at work)
    Includes index.
    ISBN 0-516-23179-0 (lib. bdg.) — ISBN 0-516-29575-6 (pbk.)
    1. Bakers and bakeries—Juvenile literature. 2. Baking—Juvenile literature. [1. Bakers
        and bakeries. 2. Occupations.] I. Title.

TX763.H883 2001
641.8'15—dc21

                                                                00-047537

62

Contents

My name is Frankie.

This is my **grandfather**.

My grandpa works in a **bakery**.

BAGELS 50¢ 55¢
PLAIN   CINNAMON RAISIN
POPPY   WILDBERRY
WHOLE WHEAT   MULTI GRAIN
SE...
ON...   EVERYTHING

nut-Butter Cookie $1.40

Nut Roll $1.95

Baklava $2.00

Elephant Ears 85¢

CRUMB BUN $1.40

Cherry Turnover $1.95

Apple Turnover $1.95

7

Grandpa **bakes** bread every morning.

9

Then he opens the bakery.

People come in to buy
bread and rolls.

11

The bread is **fresh** and warm.

It smells good.

Some people buy muffins.

The muffins are sweet and **chewy**.

15

Grandpa sells cookies and cakes, too.

Is it your **birthday**?

Grandpa will write your name on your cake!

17

People pay Grandpa.

I hand them what they buy.

Working in a bakery is hard work.

But tasting is fun!

21

New Words

bakery (**bay**-kuhr-ee) a place where breads and cakes are made and sold

bakes (**bayks**) to cook food in an oven

birthday (**berth**-day) the day you were born

chewy (**choo**-ee) when food must be chewed a lot

fresh (**frehsh**) just made; new

grandfather (**grand**-fah-thuhr) the father of your mother or father

To Find Out More

Books
At the Bakery
by Carol Greene
The Child's World

Bruno the Baker
by Lars Klinting
Henry Holt & Company

Web Site
ABC Cookie Bakers
http://www.girlscoutcookiesabc.com/pages/abfs/abfs_baker.html
On this Web site, you can take a tour of a cookie factory.

Index

About the Author

Sarah Hughes is from New York City and taught school for twelve years. She is now writing and editing children's books. In her free time she enjoys running and riding her bike.

Reading Consultants

Kris Flynn, Coordinator, Small School District Literacy, The San Diego County Office of Education

Shelly Forys, Certified Reading Recovery Specialist, W.J. Zahnow Elementary School, Waterloo, IL

Sue McAdams, Certified Reading Recovery Specialist and Literary Consultant, Dallas, TX